Dear Bá

Than

the wonderg

Love Cherie

i

Pumpkin Patch

Proverbs

&

Pies

Cherie Brooks Reilly

Recipe Editor: Bea Statz

Illustrated by: Carol Stavish

ISBN 1-57166-198-0

The Seeds for This Book

Nestled in the hills along the Ohio River in the southwestern corner of Pennsylvania is Reilly's "Summer Seat" Farm. This picturesque farm came into existence in 1983 when Lt. Col. Michael Reilly retired from the Marine Corps and bought his father's acreage with the dream of making it into a productive farm that would support his family of six. The experience of creating and living on a farm in rural suburbia and selling products directly to the public presented many challenges for Mike, myself and our four children -- Renee, Michael, Kevin, and Shawn.

This book is dedicated to my hard-working husband, Michael, and our four wonderful children; and to my dear mother, Marian Brooks, who encouraged me to write about these experiences.

A special thank you goes to Bea Statz who organized the many recipes, and to Professor Carol Stavish for her lovely illustrations.

The generous Pumpkin Patch owners who shared their favorite recipes also have my heartfelt gratitude.

THE HUMBLE PUMPKIN

The humble pumpkin has become the traditional symbol of Autumn in America. The big orange-colored stock pumpkin was brought to a high degree of perfection by the Native Americans before the European settlers arrived, and it was shared at the first Thanksgiving feast. It's nutritious flesh can be baked, boiled, fried, sauteed and pureed to make innumerable delicacies which serve as appetizers, soups, main dishes, and desserts. There's nothing like a warm bowl of pumpkin soup to chase away the Autumn chill or a spicy pumpkin pie with a dollop of whipped cream to complete a feast!

The birthplace of the pumpkin is fondly known as the "Pumpkin Patch," and it has become a favorite fall playground to which millions of families flock each year to find their perfect pumpkin for carving or eating. In the vine-laden fields, people can experience their own "roots," since the American Revolution was launched by a small nation of embattled farmers. Even at the turn of the last century, about half the population made a living from the land. Small wonder that a multitude of basic truths can be learned from a pumpkin patch, and a cornucopia of treasures and treats can be harvested!

The author of this book, Cherie Reilly, a former teacher who currently lives on a pumpkin farm in western Pennsylvania, has gathered stories about incidents that occurred on her family's pumpkin farm that testify to the fact that ancient wisdom is relearned every day, often in the most or-dinary circumstances. A librarian and cookbook author, Bea Statz, from rural Wisconsin has edited recipes that were gathered from pumpkin farmers across the nation, utilizing this truly remarkable American vegetable. The whimsical patch-work quilt illustrations by Carol Stavish, an assistant college professor, bring the Pumpkin Patch to life. Together they have created "Pumpkin Patch Proverbs and Pies" in an effort to increase appreciation for and provide insight into the worth of the humble pumpkin and its birthplace.

CHAPTERS & RECIPES

Illustration information
Pages 147-148

List of Contributors of
Pumpkin Patch Recipes
Pages 149-150

How Do You Choose a Pumpkin?

CHAPTER ONE PROVERB

"Beauty is in the eye of the Beholder"

Theocritus

Recipes

Simply Delicious Pies

*Instead of big Pumpkin-seed tears of sadness
there will be tears of joy
when you serve these easy-to-make pies.*

Note: In this book both home-cooked pumpkin pulp and purchased canned pumpkin pulp are both described in the ingredients as "**pure pumpkin**". Both forms can be used interchangeably.

When a recipe calls for a purchased can of "**pumpkin pie mix**", note that sugar and spices are already added to this. If pure pumpkin is substituted in these recipes the ingredients will need to be adjusted as indicated.

- - - - CHAPTER ONE - - - -

How Do You Choose a Pumpkin?

first noticed her when she lifted her two small children onto the wagon next to my grandchildren and me. With several other families aboard, we settled down on the sweet-smelling hay for a ride to the Pumpkin Patch. The young mother clutched her youngsters tightly as the big green tractor jerked to a start and the wagon creaked slowly down the dusty road. She exclaimed about the beauty of the colors as we passed the red and gold maple trees waving a warm October welcome.

I admired her spirit because I knew that it would have been much easier to simply buy a pumpkin at the grocery store. Instead, she had chosen to make it a special occasion.

Everyone oohed and aahed when the wagon rounded a bend and the pumpkin field came into view. Pumpkins of numerous sizes, colors, and varieties lay nestled in the curly vines among the browning leaves -- large deep-orange Howdens and Jumping Jacks, mid-sized Autumn Golds, Spookies and Harvest Moons, plump little

Baby Pams and Sugar Pies, and miniature Baby Bears.

Excited children and their parents scattered merrily across the field to seek out their special pumpkins as soon as the wagon halted. As I helped my grandchildren, Ryan and Katie, off the wagon, I saw the young woman load her baby in her backpack, and set off across the field with her toddler in tow.

Guided by instructions that they must carry their own pumpkins, four-year-old Ryan and two-year-old Katie quickly made their choices. A Sugar Pie and a Baby Bear pumpkin would do nicely and they cradled them in their arms as we caught the next wagon back to the weigh station beside the turn-of-the-century barn. As soon as we arrived, their mother whisked them off to ride the ponies.

About an hour later, I decided to take another wagon ride around the field to make certain that everything was running smoothly. As the wagon lumbered past the Pumpkin Patch, I saw the same young woman with her two small children, looking a bit weary, still wandering around among the pumpkins. At first I was a little concerned that they might have lost something; but since they didn't look unhappy, I decided that they were merely having a difficult time making a decision.

When the wagon stopped at the weigh station, I disembarked and began to help with the weighing process in order to give the staff a needed break. After guessing the weight, the smiling parents and children put their chosen pumpkins on my scale and began planning the types of decorations that they were going to make from their new prize possessions. As I weighed pumpkins and listened to detailed descriptions of Jack-O'-Lanterns-to-be, I saw the young woman with her two children climb off the wagon with a strange looking, pear-shaped pumpkin under her arm. She looked exhausted but content.

With all the perfectly-shaped beautiful pumpkins in the Patch, why did she choose that one? I wondered.

When the young woman put the odd-shaped pumpkin on my scale, my curiosity overwhelmed me. "That's an interesting pumpkin that you have there," I commented, hoping for an explanation.

"Isn't it beautiful," she beamed. "It's exactly the one that I was looking for! When I was a little girl, I read a story about Raggedy Ann and Andy; and in the story, they found a poor little pear-shaped pumpkin crying in the Pumpkin Patch. It was crying big pumpkin-seed tears because nobody wanted it. Of course, Raggedy Ann and Andy took it home and made it very happy. I was so glad to find this one out in your Pumpkin Patch!"

How do you choose a Pumpkin?
You choose a Pumpkin with your heart.

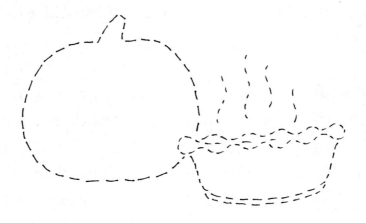

**Contributed by
Teresa Schmitt,
F & W Schmitt
Pumpkin Farm**
Long Island, NY

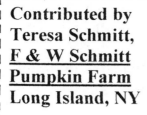

*Recipe from a
Pumpkin Patch
in New York*

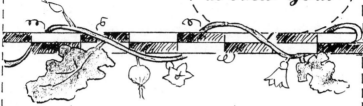

GOLDEN PUMPKIN PIE
(6 to 8 servings)

1 unbaked 9 inch pie shell
3 cups pure pumpkin
½ cup granulated sugar
2 tablespoon all-purpose flour
1 teaspoon cinnamon
½ teaspoon salt
1 ½ cups evaporated milk
        (12 ounce can)
2 eggs, well beaten

(Continued on next page)

In a saucepan, heat pumpkin over medium heat for 10 minutes, stirring frequently. In a separate bowl combine sugar, flour, cinnamon, and salt. Stir into heated pumpkin mixture. Stir milk into beaten eggs and beat into pumpkin mixture.

Pour into pie shell. Bake in preheated oven at 425 degrees for 40 minutes or until a silver knife inserted in center comes out clean.

Teresa Schmitt's family prefers the true pumpkin flavor, without much spice added. (Add ¼ teaspoon nutmeg and ¼ teaspoon ginger for a spicier pie.)

**Contributed by
Mary Jacobson,
<u>Pine Tree
Apple Orchard</u>,
White Bear Lake**

*Recipe from a
Pumpkin Patch
in Minnesota*

MOM JACOBSON'S PUMPKIN PIE
(8 servings)

1 unbaked 9-inch pie shell
1 ¾ cups pure pumpkin
1 ¾ cups evaporated milk
3 eggs
¾ cup brown sugar, packed
1 teaspoon cinnamon
½ teaspoon ginger
½ teaspoon nutmeg
¼ teaspoon cloves
½ teaspoon salt

   In a medium size bowl, combine pumpkin,
evaporated milk, eggs, brown sugar, spices
and salt. Beat well. Pour into unbaked pie
shell. Bake in preheated oven at 400 degrees
for 45-55 minutes or until a knife inserted
1 inch from edge comes out clean. Cool.

Contributed by
Barbara Middleton
<u>**Middleton**</u>
<u>**Berry Farm**</u>
Oakland, MI

Recipe from a
Pumpkin Patch
in Michigan

PRALINE PUMPKIN PIE

<u>Pecan Mixture:</u>
2 tablespoons butter
1 tablespoon orange rind
¼ cup brown sugar
¾ cups chopped pecans

Prepare your favorite baked
pumpkin pie recipe. Combine
above ingredients and sprinkle
over pie during last 10 minutes
of baking time.

**Contributed by
Sunday Todosciuk
Andy T's Farms,
St. John's, MI**

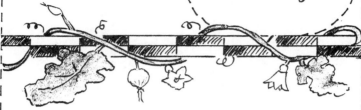

*Recipe from a
Pumpkin Patch
in Michigan*

INSTANT PUMPKIN PIE
(8 servings)

1 9-inch pie shell, baked
1 cup pure pumpkin
1 large package (6 serving size)
    instant vanilla pudding mix
1 ½ cups milk
1 teaspoon pumpkin pie spice
1 cup whipped topping

  Combine pumpkin, vanilla pudding
mix, milk, and spice in a large mixer
bowl. Beat at lowest speed for 1 minute.
Slowly add whipped topping.
  Pour into pie shell and chill 3 hours.
Garnish with additional whipped
topping and chopped pecans, if desired.

14

The Grouch

CHAPTER TWO PROVERB

"No act of kindness, no matter how small, is ever wasted"

Aesop

Recipes

Extraordinary Pumpkin Pies

Serve any of these delicious pies and all grouches will disappear.

- - - - CHAPTER TWO - - - -

The Grouch

Anyone who works with "The Public" knows that statistically, in every group of 1000 people, there will be at least one Grouch (a paranoid, unhappy person who thinks that everything is a rip-off). And even if the other 999 people are pleasant, happy and affirming, the one Grouch will ruin your day and give you acid indigestion.

In October, when thousands of people come to our farm to enjoy the harvest season, the autumn air is colored with laughter and excitement; a carnival mood prevails. However, it is inevitable that a Grouch will come, too. Unfortunately, I had never learned how to deal with grouches because critical, negative people hurt my feelings - which I have learned is actually passive anger.

Never try to please or pacify a Grouch because it only makes them grouchier. The general rule is: refrain from offering any explanation or argument, and simply listen, apologize, and give them their money back.

Many times I've longed to say, "Too expensive, Ma'am? At the movie theater you pay over twice as much to sit in the dark for an hour and witness violence, sex, profanity, and frightening images that you try to forget. But here, for much less, you can enjoy a wonderful shared adventure with your family and friends, and experience a hayride, pumpkin hunt, and ten other wonderful activities that will provide you with memories that you'll cherish for a lifetime!" Or, "You think that the hayride should be free, sir? But how will I pay for that $50,000 tractor that is pulling you on that $5,000 wagon through that multi-thousand dollar land where I have gone to a great deal of time, labor and expense to grow those pumpkins for your picking pleasure?"

The euphoria of a lovely autumn day and the flurry of fall excitement were interrupted recently by a Grouch who caught me by surprise. She was a depression-era Grouch, which are potentially the most vicious kind, since they remember pennya-loaf bread. As she was shaking her finger in my face and declaring that her grandfather's farm was free and I should be ashamed of charging so much and how I should "give all this money to charity to make amends," I suddenly did not feel like apologizing. In fact I was thinking, "Get on your broom, witch, and be gone!"

However, I remembered a theory from psychology class, and when she paused in her tirade, I looked at her with sympathetic, understanding eyes and said softly, "You must be having a very difficult day. Is there anything that I can do to help?"

Her mouth dropped in mid-sentence, and she was dumbstruck. Finally she said in a transformed manner, "My family left me on that bench over there while they went to find pumpkins because they thought the hayride would be too much for me, and my arthritis is acting up again."

"Do you have some medicine in your purse?" I asked in a concerned voice. "I'll gladly get you some water," I offered, "and there's a chair over there in the shade that would be much more comfortable."

"That would be nice," she said, and went over to sit under the tree, while I went to find a glass of water.

The last time that I saw her, she was sitting in the shade of the maple tree smiling as she watched the happy children climb aboard the haywagon for an exciting ride to the Pumpkin Patch.

PUMPKIN PATCH PROVERB:
Those who want to be loved the most,
Often act the most unlovable.

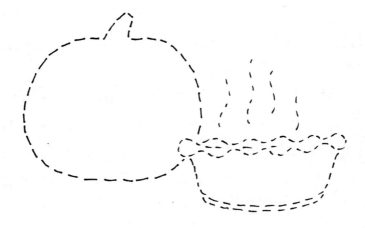

Contributed by
Helen Huitink
Pumpkinland
Orange City, IA

Recipe from a
Pumpkin Patch
in Iowa

GLORIA'S SENSATIONAL
DOUBLE LAYER PUMPKIN PIE

1 9-inch graham cracker pie crust
1 (3oz.) package of cream cheese
1 cup plus 1 tablespoons cold milk
1 tablespoon sugar
1 ½ cups thawed whipped topping
2 (3.4 oz.) packages vanilla instant
    pudding and pie filling
2 cups pure pumpkin
1 teaspoon cinnamon
½ teaspoon ground ginger
¼ teaspoon ground cloves

(Continued on next page)

Mix softened cream cheese, 1 tablespoon of milk and sugar with whisk until smooth. Gently stir in whipped topping. Spread on bottom of graham cracker crust.

Pour 1 cup milk into mixing bowl. Add pudding mix. Beat with wire whisk until blended, 1 or 2 minutes. Let stand 3 minutes. Stir in pumpkin and spices; mix well. Spread over cream cheese layer. Refrigerate at least 2 hours. Garnish with additional whipped topping and nuts, as desired. Makes 8 servings.

**Contributed by
<u>Lyman Orchards
Farm Market</u>,
Middlefield, CT.**

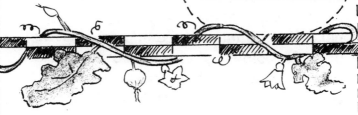

*Recipe from a
Pumpkin Patch
in Connecticut*

PUMPKIN-BANANA PIE
(Serves 8)

1 9-inch graham cracker pie shell
2 cups pure pumpkin
2 ripe bananas, mashed (¾ cup)
12 ounce can evaporated skim milk
1 egg, beaten
1 cup sugar
1 teaspoon pumpkin pie spice

(Continued on next page)

Preheat oven to 400 degrees. In a large bowl, combine bananas, pumpkin, milk, egg, sugar and pumpkin pie spice; mix well. Place pie shell on baking sheet and pour mixture into shell. Bake in preheated oven at 400 degrees for 15 minutes.

Reduce oven heat to 350 degrees and bake 40-45 minutes, or until knife inserted in center comes out clean. Cool completely on wire rack. Serve at room temperature or chilled.

Contributed by
Bea Statz(Recipe Ed.)
Statz's
Christmas Trees
Baraboo, WI

Recipe from the State of Wisconsin

CREAMY PUMPKIN RUM PIE
(8 servings)

1 baked 9-inch deep dish pie shell
2 envelopes unflavored gelatin
½ cup water
1 ¾ cup pure pumpkin
        (15 ounce can)
¾ cup brown sugar
1 cup dairy sour cream
1 teaspoon cinnamon
¼ teaspoon ginger
¼ teaspoon nutmeg
3 tablespoons rum
1 cup heavy whipping cream

(Continued on next page)

In a small saucepan, combine and stir gelatin and water over low heat until dissolved. Set aside. In a medium bowl, combine and mix pumpkin, brown sugar, sour cream, cinnamon, ginger, nutmeg and rum until smooth. Add gelatin mixture and mix until blended. Chill until mixture begins to stiffen but is not quite set. In a medium bowl, beat cream until stiff. Fold into pumpkin mixture. Turn into prepared baked pie shell. Chill for 2 to 3 hours before serving.

Cool

CHAPTER THREE PROVERB

"The only thing we have to fear is fear itself"

Franklin D. Roosevelt

Recipes

Frozen Pumpkin Treats

Everyone will agree that these treats are really cool.

- - - - CHAPTER THREE - - - -

Cool

As told by Barbara Miller

The deformed monster limped toward us, his hunched-back

form bending him to our size. I was repulsed by his scarred, warty countenance as he thrust his head in my face and said, "The ticket line is over there, ma'am".

Reilly's Pumpkin Farm was advertising SPOOKY NIGHT HAYRIDES. I had heard that it was a nice family activity that just gave you a bit of a fright, but it definitely was not one of those bloody, grotesque, vomit-inducing, horrific experiences that are so realistic that they would haunt you for weeks afterwards. So when my five-year-old son Kevin begged to go, I was ready for some fun; and happy for a chance to be a kid again, because I had many fond Halloween memories of scary things that went bump in the night.

My thirteen-year-old daughter, Amy, asked to go along; and she invited her closest friend, Nicole. Amy was at the age where she had to be totally cool and in charge; but I didn't realize that she had become so obnoxious about it.

Kevin's eyes grew wide with fascination and apprehension when he saw the gruesome attendants, but Amy just scoffed at them and declared they wouldn't scare a flea. I immediately began to regret including her in the outing.

We boarded the tractor-drawn wagon with several other people and slowly slipped into the darkness of the night. As we lumbered along the country road, two witches appeared on the left side of the hay wagon. They were bent over and intently stirring a huge, steaming cauldron fueled by a wood fire. The flames illuminated their repugnant faces and revealed that both were missing at least one front tooth. They interrupted their labors to beckon to us in a sinister manner and even staggered after us with outstretched hands, as if they desired some more ingredients for their stew. I felt a little shiver and Kevin snuggled closer to me. However, Amy declared in a know-it-all voice, "What a bunch of phonies! They really need acting lessons!"

As we continued on the hayride, her cool comments became more and more annoying, and her derogatory remarks were beginning to dispel the spooky mood and spoil our good time. I was about to tell her to keep her comments to herself when oozing out of the darkness came a shadowy figure.

It mounted the running board of our wagon, directly behind where Amy and her friend were leaning against the side. I sat transfixed as a black-gloved hand reached out and the fingers slowly closed around Amy's arm. When she felt something touch her arm, Amy turned with a start to determine the source; and there, looming over her in the darkness, was a menacing, black-shrouded figure.

A shriek pierced the night air as Amy scrambled across the wagon on all fours, dragging Nicole with her. The dark figure disappeared into the night as quickly as it had appeared, leaving us to wonder if we had really witnessed the apparition.

However, it left a lasting impression on Amy and Nicole who sat motionless and breathless for a moment as if bewitched. Finally, an obviously stunned Amy declared, "That was weird!"

Assuming positions in the middle of the wagon, the two friends spent the rest of the ride looking tentatively over each other's shoulder. Kevin and I settled down to enjoy the rest of the ride and feel the little tingles of fear tip-toe up our backbones as we passed strange creatures and spooky scenes. I chuckled to myself and wondered if the apparition had really been my guardian angel in disguise.

PUMPKIN PATCH PROVERBIAL CONTRADICTION:

The Icy Fingers of Fear Melt Cool.

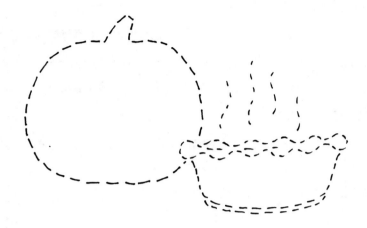

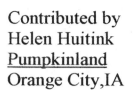

Contributed by
Helen Huitink
<u>Pumpkinland</u>
Orange City,IA

Recipe from a
Pumpkin Patch
in Iowa

PUMPKIN ICE CREAM PIE
WITH CARAMEL PECAN SAUCE

<u>Crust:</u>
1 ½ cups crushed gingersnap cookies
      (about 30)
¼ cup butter, melted
<u>Filling:</u>
½ teaspoon cinnamon
1 pint vanilla ice cream (softened)
¾ cup brown sugar (packed)
½ teaspoon ginger
½ teaspoon cinnamon
¼ teaspoon cloves
1 cup pure pumpkin
1 cup whipping cream
<u>Sauce:</u>
1 cup caramel ice cream topping
½ cup chopped pecans

(Continued)

In small bowl, combine crust ingredients; blend well. Press firmly in bottom and up sides of 9-inch pie pan. Refrigerate 15 min.

Meanwhile, in large bowl, stir ½ teaspoon cinnamon into ice cream. Spoon into crust. Freeze.

In medium bowl, combine brown sugar, ginger, ½ teaspoon cinnamon, cloves, and pumpkin: blend well. Fold in whipped cream. Spoon over ice cream in crust. Freeze 3 hours until firm. Let stand at room temperature 20 min. before serving.

In small saucepan, combine caramel topping and pecans. Cook over medium heat until thoroughly heated, stirring constantly. Serve warm over pie. Makes 8-10 servings.

Helen and her sister, Gloria Patterson, have a wonderful cookbook called PUMPKINLAND PUMPKIN COOKBOOK available at Dave and Helen's farm.

**Contributed by
Sunday Todosciuk
<u>Andy T's Farms</u>
St. Johns, MI**

*Recipe from a
Pumpkin Patch
in Michigan*

PUMPKIN ICE CREAM
(10 servings)

2 cups milk
2 cups pure pumpkin
4 egg yolks **or** 2 eggs, beaten
1 cup sugar
2 teaspoon cinnamon
1 teaspoon nutmeg
½ teaspoon allspice
¼ teaspoon ginger
1/8 teaspoon salt
½ teaspoon vanilla extract
1 cup whipping cream (optional)
1 cup chopped pecans or walnuts
(optional)

(Continued on next page)

In a double boiler, bring milk to a scald stage. In a large bowl, combine and mix pumpkin, eggs, sugar, cinnamon, nutmeg, allspice, ginger, and salt. Slowly stir mixture into milk. Cook 4 minutes longer, stirring constantly until thickened. Add vanilla and remove from double boiler. Cool one hour in refrigerator. Add and stir in cream and nuts. Pour into ice cream freezer container. Crank until stiff following freezer instructions.

Contributed by
Cherie Reilly
Reilly's
Summer Seat Farm
Pittsburgh, PA

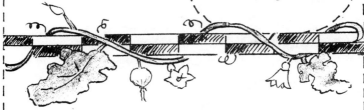

Recipe from a
Pumpkin Patch
in Pennsylvania

CRUNCHY FROZEN
PUMPKIN SQUARES
(serves approx.16 people)

Crumb crust:
1 box yellow cake mix
½ cup macadamia nuts
½ cup butter or margarine

Combine ingredients in a medium bowl until crumbly. Pour into ungreased 13x9 inch baking pan. Bake in preheated oven at 350 degrees for 15 minutes. Stir mixture and bake another 5 to 10 minutes or until slightly browned. Crumble the crumb mixture

(Continued on next page)

Remove 1 ½ cup of crumb mixture
from pan to reserve for topping. Pat
remaining crumbs evenly in pan. Cool.

Filling:
1 to 2 teaspoons cinnamon
½ teaspoon salt
2 cups miniature marshmallows
1 ¾ cups pumpkin pie mix
2 crumbled Heath candy bars
½ gallon vanilla ice cream, softened
1 cup coconut

Combine Filling ingredients and pour
over cooled crumb mixture in pan.
Sprinkle with reserved 1½ cups of crumb
mixture and ½ cup pecans. Freeze until
solid. Remove from freezer ½ hour before
cutting into squares for serving.

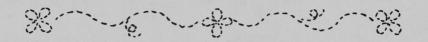

Choices

CHAPTER FOUR PROVERB

"Trust Each Other"
Marriage Encounter

Recipes

Choice Pumpkin Desserts

*Everyone will choose these desserts
as their favorites.*

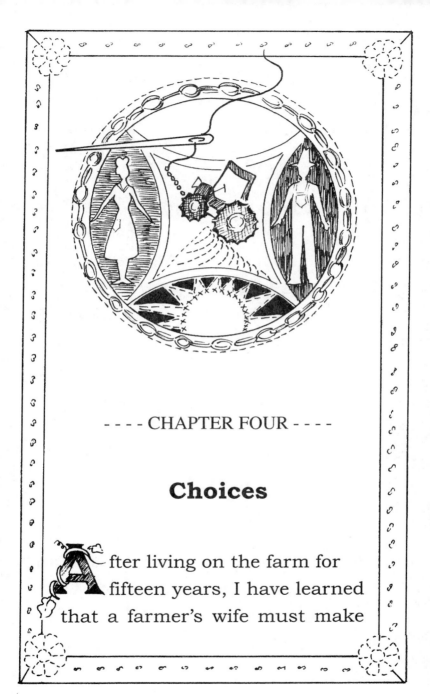

- - - - CHAPTER FOUR - - - -

Choices

After living on the farm for fifteen years, I have learned that a farmer's wife must make choices that are not always as simple as which pair of blue jeans to wear, or what to make for dinner. In fact, some decisions can be quite weighty. For instance, one rainy day my husband, Mike, poked his head in the farmhouse door and asked me to come and help him. I slipped on my raincoat and old sneakers and followed him to the area where he had been leveling a part of the hillside with our new blue tractor. He had been pushing dirt over an embankment in order to make way for a new fence.

When we reached the area where he had been working, I understood why he needed help. The blue tractor was perched precariously at the edge of a 10-foot drop-off. The rain had made the clay soil very slippery. As he had maneuvered the tractor to push the dirt over the edge, the tractor had slipped too far down the hill and the more that he tried to maneuver it back up the slope, the closer it slid toward the abyss. He realized that the situation was impossible to resolve alone so he had carefully set the hand brake and went to fetch the 85-horsepower green tractor and me.

Carefully he connected the two tractors with a long chain. Then he turned to me and said, "O.K., you can choose which tractor you want to drive."

"This is a choice?" I muttered in horror.

I could climb on the blue tractor, release the hand brake and plummet to my death; or I could climb on the green tractor and if I didn't shift the gears correctly and release the clutch at the right time and speed to keep the chain taunt, I could send my husband plunging over the precipice.

I looked at both tractors. I hated to get on the blue one for it appeared to be hanging by a thread. I looked longingly at the green tractor sitting a safe distance away and considered my tractor-driving skills. I recalled that two years ago, while I was driving the small Kaboda tractor, I had chosen the wrong path across the field. The little tractor had slid down the hillside and tipped over on its side. Fortunately, it had eased over slowly and there was a roll bar on it, so I wasn't hurt; but it dampened my enthusiasm for tractor driving. I realized that in this situation all would be better served if I chose the blue tractor.

Slowly I mounted the steps to the cab of the blue tractor, being careful not to jiggle anything. I sat apprehensively in the big seat surrounded by levers and brakes. Mike set the gears and explained exactly what I must do -- release the hand brake and let the clutch out very slowly at the precise moment that I felt the chains pulling the tractor backwards.

As I sat there waiting to feel the tug, I prayed, "Oh God, can I do this?"

I could, I did, and it worked. As I climbed down the steps from the cab, my knees were trembling, and I said a little thank-you prayer as I touched solid ground.

Mike came toward me with a smile and said, "Good choice!"

I knew by the twinkle in his eye that he knew there never really was a choice, and I loved him for letting me make it.

PUMPKIN PATCH PROVERB:
>The Beauty of a Choice
>is in the Eye of the Chooser.

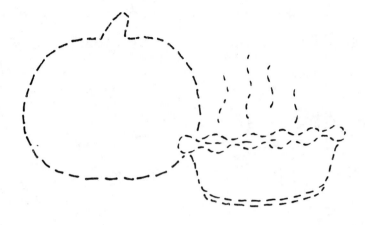

**Contributed by
Linda Struye,
<u>The Little Farmer</u>
Malone, WI**

*Recipe from a
Pumpkin Patch
in Wisconsin*

THE BIG PUMPKIN BRULEE
(6-8 servings)

1 ¾ cups half and half cream
¾ cup sugar
2 tablespoons butter at room temp.
6 slices cinnamon raisin bread
¾ cup pure pumpkin
4 egg yolks
1 egg
1 tablespoon Kahlúa
1 teaspoon vanilla extract
¼ teaspoon ground nutmeg
¼ teaspoon cinnamon
¼ teaspoon salt

6 tablespoon whipping cream
6 tablespoons brown sugar

(Continued on next page)

Stir half and half and sugar in medium saucepan and cook over medium heat until sugar dissolves. Remove from heat and cool to lukewarm.

Spread butter over 1 side of each bread slice. Cut bread into ¾ inch square pieces. Pour into large (25 cm) glass pie plate. Whisk pumpkin, egg yolks, egg, and flavorings. In medium bowl until blended. Add half and half mixture and whisk smooth. Pour pumpkin custard mixture over bread cubes. Let stand 30 minutes, occasionally pressing on bread to submerge.

Preheat oven to 350 degrees. Place glass pie plate in large roasting pan. Add hot water into pan to come half way up the sides of the pie plate. Tent entire pan loosely with foil.

Place in preheated oven and bake 60-65 minutes or until knife inserted in center comes out clean. Remove from oven and completely cool on rack. Cover and refrigerate at least 4 hours or overnight.

Preheat broiler. Spoon the whipping cream over the top the Big Brulee. Sprinkle with brown sugar. Broil 2 minutes or until top is bubbly and golden brown, watching closely. Cut into 6-8 pieces and serve immediately.

Contributed by
Carolyn Beinlich
Triple B Farms
Monongahela, Pa.

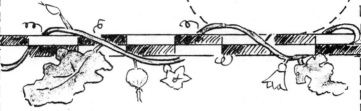

Recipe from a Pumpkin Patch in Pennsylvania

CAROLYN'S PUMPKIN COBBLER
(Crust mixture rises to the top during baking to form a delicious topping.)

FILLING:
2 eggs
1 cup evaporated milk
3 cups pure pumpkin
1 cup white sugar
½ cup brown sugar
1 tablespoon flour
1 teaspoon cinnamon
¼ teaspoon ginger
¼ teaspoon cloves
¼ teaspoon nutmeg
½ teaspoon salt

(continued on next page)

CRUST:
½ cup butter
1 cup flour
1 cup white sugar
4 teaspoon baking power
½ teaspoon salt
1 cup reg. or low-fat milk
1 teaspoon vanilla

TOPPING:
1 tablespoon butter
2 tablespoons white sugar

Preheat oven to 350 degrees F. In a large bowl, combine eggs, milk, and pumpkin. Add rest of FILLING ingredients, mix well and set aside.

To prepare crust, melt butter in 9x11 inch baking pan. In another bowl, mix other CRUST ingredients until just combined and pour into baking pan on top of melted butter. Spoon or pour filling evenly over crust batter in pan. DO NOT STIR. Dot top with remaining butter and sprinkle with remaining sugar. Bake 1 hour. Serves 8-10 people.

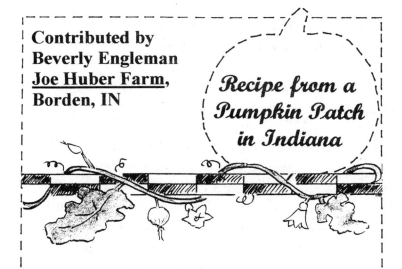

*Recipe from a
Pumpkin Patch
in Indiana*

PUMPKIN ROLL
(Serves 12)

3 eggs
1 cup sugar
¾ cup pure pumpkin
1 tablespoon lemon juice
¾ cup all purpose flour
1 teaspoon baking powder
2 teaspoons cinnamon
½ teaspoon ginger
½ teaspoon salt
1 cup nuts, chopped

(Direction on next page)

In a mixing bowl, beat eggs until thick. Gradually beat in sugar. Add lemon juice and pumpkin.

In a separate bowl, sift together flour, baking powder, spices and salt. Slowly add flour mixture to pumpkin mixture. Pour batter into a greased and floured jelly roll pan and spread evenly. Sprinkle nuts over batter.

Bake in a preheated oven at 375 degrees for 15 minutes or until toothpick comes out clean. Sprinkle a towel with powdered sugar and after cooling slightly, turn the baked roll over on the towel, Roll up and let cool.

Unroll and spread filling on cake, rolling again after filling is added.

Filling:
1 8-ounce package cream cheese
4 tablespoon butter
½ teaspoon vanilla extract
1 cup powdered sugar

Mix all ingredients until smooth and spread evenly on cake. Store in refrigerator.

Sir Thomas Turkey, Esquire

CHAPTER FIVE PROVERB

"For Everything there is a season, a time for every purpose under the Heaven..."

The Bible

Recipes

Favorite Pumpkin Breads

You can strut up and down in your most regal fashion after making these delicious breads, knowing that you're efforts will be appreciated.

- - - - CHAPTER FIVE - - - -

SIR THOMAS TURKEY, ESQUIRE

My friend, Linda, reached over the barnyard fence and petted the nose of our black and white cow. Casually she inquired, "Do you have a name for your cow?"

"Filet Mignon IV," came the reply.

She paled a bit at the implication and then mused, "I'm not sure that I could eat an animal that I had come to know personally."

I smiled as I thought of how far I had come in accepting the practicalities of farm life. When I first arrived at the farm I, too, had found it difficult to come to grips with the concept of eating pets. However, things came into perspective because of an incident that occurred after our third year in the country.

The most enjoyable activities during the month of October are the children's school tours. Exuberant children scour the Pumpkin Patch to find their own special pumpkin. Much deep contemplation and careful searching goes into their selection and by the end of the season, not a single untrodden corner remains in any of the fields.

The tour culminates in a delightful visit with the farm animals. Beside the weathered barn is a woven-wire animal enclosure, where the children and animals gather and peek curiously at each other through the square openings of the fence. After learning how to flatten the palm of their hand to feed the cow, calf, sheep and goats, the youngsters eagerly clamor for kernels of corn and giggle with delight as the animals tickle their hands while lapping up the grains. The children also receive corn to throw on the ground for the chickens, turkeys, and ducks to peck and the pig to scoop up.

One turkey was especially grateful for the treats. He would spread his tail feathers into an enormous fan, stiffen his wings so that the tips scraped along the ground with a clucking noise, and strut up and down in front of the children in his most regal fashion. As he strutted by, the children would reach out their tiny fingers to touch his iridescent brown feathers, and their eyes would grow wide with wonder at the splendor of this marvelous creature. I loved his showmanship and style, and when Thanksgiving time approached, I let it be known that he was not to be considered for the main course.

About two months after Sir Thomas Turkey had been granted everlasting life by his master, a dreadful, mind-altering incident occurred. Our family had gone away for the day, and when we returned and entered the driveway to the house, I was horrified to see pieces of Sir Thomas scattered about the yard. Feathers floated in the air, Sir Thomas' mangled and broken body lay beside the road, and wing tips and drumsticks were scattered up the hillside. It was apparent that Sir Thomas had died a frightening and cruel death, probably at the jaws of one of the stray dogs that occasionally invaded our farm.

I wept remorseful tears when I realized that my "kindness" had caused this heart-rending scene. How much kinder the quick chop of the axe would have been! This wonderful animal deserved a painless, dignified death because he had lived so gracefully. It was then that I resolved to put sentimentality aside and accept the fact that every creature has its season. After all, death is inevitable. The best reward for a life well-lived is a quick, painless, dignified death; and I hope that my own season will end in such a manner. Now, when Thanksgiving comes around, I simply declare, "Off with his head and on with the feast! It's time!"

I suppose if there is a lesson to be learned from this occurrence, it might be: Never fall in love with a turkey (which, after all, is very sage advice).

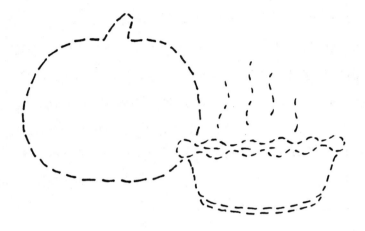

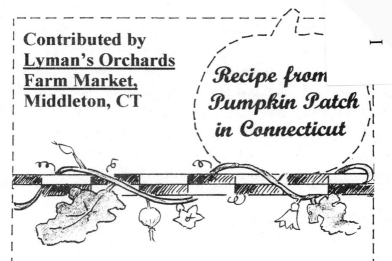

*Recipe from
Pumpkin Patch
in Connecticut*

PUMPKIN-APPLE MUFFINS
(24 muffins)

2 ½ cups flour
1 ½ cups sugar
1 tablespoon pumpkin pie spice
1 teaspoon baking soda
½ teaspoon salt
2 eggs
1 cup pure pumpkin
½ cup vegetable oil
2 cups chopped apples
½ cup chopped nuts (optional)

(Continued on next page)

a large bowl, sift together flour, sugar, pie spice, baking soda and salt. In a separate bowl, beat eggs well. Add pumpkin and oil to eggs, mixing well. Make a well in the center of the flour mixture and add pumpkin mixture. Stir until moistened. Add apples and nuts. Spoon batter into lined muffin pans. Bake in pre-heated oven at 350 degrees for 35-40 minutes.

Optional Topping:
4 tablespoon flour
½ cup sugar
1 teaspoon cinnamon
8 teaspoon butter

Combine flour, sugar and cinnamon. Cut in butter until crumbly. Sprinkle over top of muffins in pan before baking.

**Contributed by
The Trax Family
<u>Trax Farms, Inc.</u>
Finleyville, PA**

*Recipe from a
Pumpkin Patch
in Pennsylvania*

PUMPKIN RIBBON BREAD

<u>Filling:</u>
2 pkgs. (8 oz.) cream cheese, softened
1/3 cup sugar
1 tablespoon flour
1 egg
2 teaspoons grated orange peel

<u>Bread:</u>
1 cup pure pumpkin
½ cup vegetable oil
2 eggs
1½ cups sugar
½ teaspoon salt
½ teaspoon cloves
½ teaspoon cinnamon
1-2/3 cups flour
1 teaspoon baking soda
1 cup chopped pecans

For **Filling,** beat cream cheese, sugar, and flour together in a small bowl. Add egg; mix to blend. Stir in orange peel; set aside. Make **Bread** by combining pumpkin, oil and eggs in a large bowl. Add sugar, salt, cloves, cinnamon, flour, baking soda, and pecans: mix to blend. Pour ¼ of batter into 2 greased and floured 7 1/2 X 3 1/3 X 3 inch loaf pans. Carefully spread the cream cheese mixture over the batter. Add the remaining batter to cover filling. Bake in preheated 325 degree oven for 1 ½ hours or until bread tests done with a wooden pick. Cool for 10 minutes before removing from the pans. Store in refrigerator. Makes two loaves.

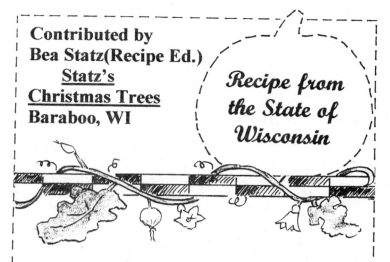

PUMPKIN HONEY MUFFINS
(12 servings)

1 cup pure pumpkin
1 cup honey
¼ cup vegetable oil
2 eggs, lightly beaten
¼ cup low-fat buttermilk
1 teaspoon vanilla extract
2 cups all-purpose flour
1 ½ tablespoon ground cinnamon
1 teaspoon baking soda
½ teaspoon salt
½ cup walnuts or pecans, chopped

(Continued on next page)

In a medium bowl, blend pumpkin, honey, oil, eggs, buttermilk and vanilla until smooth. In a large bowl, sift together flour, cinnamon, baking soda and salt; stir in nuts. Pour pumpkin mixture over dry ingredients. Stir until just mixed. Spoon batter into paper-lined or greased muffin tin, filling each ¾ full.

Bake in preheated 350 degree F. oven for 25 minutes or until toothpick inserted in center of muffins comes out clean. Let cool on rack five minutes. Remove muffins from pan and let cool on rack completely.

Cream cheese frosting (optional)
8 ounces cream cheese, softened
1/3 cup honey
In a small bowl, with electric mixer, beat cream cheese and honey. Frost muffins, after they cool.

Note: Can add ½ cup raisins, craisins or dates .

The King of Obstinacy

CHAPTER SIX PROVERB

"Speak Softly,
and Carry a Big Stick"
Theodore Roosevelt

Recipes

Chewy Pumpkin Bars

*Even the most obstinate individual
will have to admit these bars are delicious.*

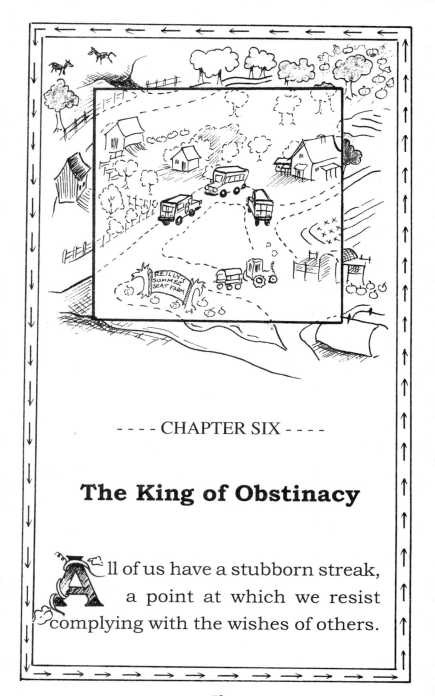

- - - - CHAPTER SIX - - - -

The King of Obstinacy

All of us have a stubborn streak, a point at which we resist complying with the wishes of others.

Usually an understanding can be reached that will satisfy both sides, and each side will give a little ground in order to serve a greater good. Finding that point of compromise with some individuals can be excruciatingly difficult, and sometimes seemingly impossible, as I discovered one fateful day in October.

Each Autumn the peaceful rural atmosphere is electrified by the sound of children coming and going as school classes invade the countryside for a farm field trip. Shortly after school convenes in the morning, the big yellow school buses begin to roar down our country road, bringing youngsters to our pumpkin farm; and they continue throughout the day until about an hour before the dismissal bell.

The teachers and buses are usually on a tight schedule so it is important that the process of loading and unloading the children runs smoothly. Over the years we have developed a very effective circular traffic pattern which facilitates the logistics of the school tours. The buses enter our farm gate and turn to the right toward the market area where the children disembark. After the teacher has paid for the tour and received plastic pumpkin bags, the children and teacher climb aboard the hay wagon and the tractor driver transports them to the "Little Pumpkin Patch" bursting with Sugar Pie pumpkins.

Upon arriving at the field, the driver helps the classes off the wagon and shows them the point at the far end of the field where they will be picked up for the return trip. Whereupon the children scatter, joyfully running from pumpkin to pumpkin, examining this one and that one until they finally make their selection. After popping their prize into their bags, they scurry toward the pick-up point to wait for their teacher and classmates, possibly exchanging their pumpkin along the way for a more fetching one. Most of the children are in preschool or the primary grades and the smaller Sugar Pie pumpkins are the perfect size for them to carry as they explore the cornstalk maze and feed the farm animals when the pumpkin treasure-hunt is over.

While this is happening in the field, the bus driver who delivered the teacher and students to the hayride staging area continues to drive the bus to the left around a narrow circular road carved out of the side of the hill. At the end of a semi-circle and directly below the animal enclosure, each driver parks his bus on the road, and waits for his students to complete the tour and climb aboard the bus again.

We were pleased with the efficiency of the traffic pattern, and oftentimes as many as five or six buses would be neatly arranged in a row along the single-lane road, waiting to whisk their students back to class. As soon as the lead bus departed for school the next bus would move up to the ready position and open its doors. We marveled at the clock-like precision which governed the motion of the buses.

One cloudy day, a school bus pulled into our driveway and turned <u>left</u> instead of right. The driver traveled down the out road and came to rest nose-to-nose with the first bus in the bus line. The driver opened the door and unceremoniously discharged his teachers and students, causing them to walk across the small grassy field to get to the market area, where they were to board the hay wagons. My tractor-driving brother, Dale, who was waiting for his wagon to be filled with children, saw a problem developing and said, "I'll go and talk to the guy."

Five minutes later he returned shaking his head and said, "I explained things to him, I tried to reason with him, and I even begged him to move, but that guy is some kind of stubborn! Go and see what you can do. I have to get these kids out to the pumpkin field."

I glanced at the bus line and saw another bus driver walk toward the backward bus. He leaned his head in the door and talked to the driver. Holding my breath, I waited with crossed fingers hoping he would resolve the problem, but the man soon turned and went back to his own vehicle.

Children carrying pumpkins were beginning to come down the hill to board the right-way bus, and I felt impending doom. Deciding that it was time for a woman's touch, I scurried across the field toward the bus. Smilingly, I mounted the steps of the bus and said in a pleasant tone, "Excuse me, sir, but you're in the wrong place and these other buses will have to leave very soon."

I barely got the words out of my mouth when he declared gruffly, "Well, there's no sign telling me not to be here, so I'm staying right where I am."

I could feel my anger rising and decided a more stern approach was needed. "Sir, if you don't move this bus, I'll have to call the police!" I said, knowing in my heart of hearts that would probably take a long time.

That statement really provoked his anger. He set his jaw, folded his arms, leaned back in his seat and closed his eyes as if he were going to sleep! The King of Obstinacy had called my bluff and was royally dismissing me!

I was at a loss for words -- at least helpful, constructive ones, so I backed out of the door. Once out of the bus, I noticed that the right-way bus was loaded and ready to go. I could envision the tardy buses, the irate teachers, and the angry parents if those students didn't get back to school by the scheduled time. Things looked bleak.

Fortunately, I was born in the era when women didn't have to solve all their own problems. In fact, my motto has always been, "When the going gets tough, the tough get their husbands." Instinctively I looked around for Mike and noticed that he had just pulled his tractor into the loading area. I ran across the field as fast as my unliberated legs could carry me and signaled for him to come down from the tractor cab. Quickly, I described the crisis, using the words rude and obstinate in the description. Mike scowled and headed across the field. I could tell by his George S. Patton strides that he was on a mission.

Mike stomped up the steps of the bus, leaned over the reclining bus driver and said, "Get this ##*!!!**## bus out of here, or I'll wrap a log chain around your rear axle and pull you out of the way!!!!"

That got the King's attention. Whether he had a sudden change of heart, or whether the humiliating image of being dragged helplessly backwards in his big yellow bus moved him, he began casting about for a way to save face.

"Well," he whined, "I just wanted someone to show me a little respect."

Mike straightened up, replaced the scowl on his face with a smile, and said softly, "Please."

The driver reached down for his key. Mike stepped off the bus, and the beeping behemoth slowly backed out of the driveway. The bus filled with antsy children that had been waiting, began lumbering down the driveway and headed back to school.

The errant bus driver waited unobtrusively for his charges to return, and when they appeared all excited and loaded with pumpkins, he welcomed them with open doors and hurried them back to class.

The next day we posted "Do Not Enter" signs on the left side of the driveway, and the traffic has been flowing freely ever since.

PUMPKIN PATCH PROVERB:
Speak Softly, But Have a Big Tractor.

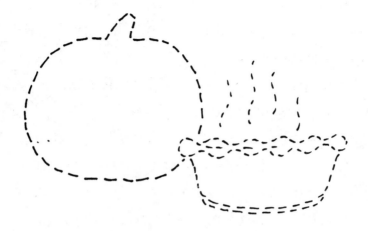

Contributed by
Susan Butler,
Butler's Orchard,
Germantown, MD

Recipe from a
Pumpkin Patch
in Maryland

BUTLER'S PUMPKIN BARS
(24 bars)

2 cups all-purpose flour
2 teaspoons baking powder
1 teaspoon baking soda
½ teaspoon salt
2 teaspoons cinnamon
4 beaten eggs
1 cup oil
1 ½ cups sugar
2 cups pure pumpkin

In a large bowl, sift together flour,
baking powder, baking soda, salt, and
cinnamon.

(Continued on next page)

In separate bowl, beat eggs. Add sugar, oil, and pumpkin; mixing well. Add flour mixture to pumpkin mixture; mixing well.

Pour into 10x15x1inch greased jelly roll pan. Bake in preheated oven at 350 degrees for 25 minutes. Cool.

Frosting:
1 8-ounce package cream cheese
¼ cup butter
2 cups sifted powdered sugar
1 teaspoon vanilla extract
Chopped nuts

In a medium-size mixer bowl, cream together cream cheese and butter. Mix in powdered sugar and vanilla. Beat until smooth and spread over cooled bars. Cut into bars. Sprinkle with chopped nuts, if desired.

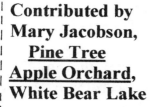

*Recipe from a
Pumpkin Patch
in Minnesota*

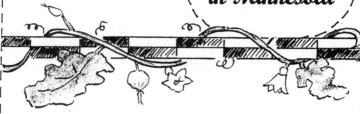

MARY'S PUMPKIN BARS
(24 bars)

2 cups pure pumpkin
4 eggs
2 cups sugar
1 cup oil

    In a medium bowl, mix together pumpkin, eggs, sugar and oil. Set aside.

2 cups flour
2 teaspoons baking powder
1 teaspoon baking soda
2 teaspoons ground cinnamon
½ teaspoon ginger
½ teaspoon nutmeg
½ teaspoon cloves
½ teaspoon salt

(Continued on next page)

In a separate bowl, sift together flour, baking powder, baking soda, and seasonings.

Slowly stir flour mixture into pumpkin mixture. Mix well. Pour into a 9x13 inch ungreased pan. Bake in a preheated oven at 350 degrees for 30 minutes or until tooth-pick inserted in center comes out clean. Remove from oven and cool before frosting.

Frosting:
3 cups powdered sugar, sifted
2 tablespoon butter, softened
1 8-ounce package cream cheese, softened
1 teaspoon vanilla extract

In a mixer bowl, combine powdered sugar, butter, cream cheese and vanilla extract. Beat on medium speed until smooth.

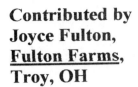

**Contributed by
Joyce Fulton,
<u>Fulton Farms</u>,
Troy, OH**

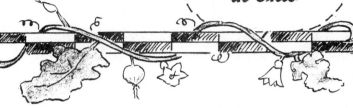

*Recipe from a
Pumpkin Patch
in Ohio*

PUMPKIN PARTY SQUARES
(24 servings)

<u>Crus</u>t:
1 cup flour
½ cup quick oatmeal
½ cup brown sugar
½ cup butter or margarine, softened

<u>Filling</u>:
2 cups pure pumpkin
2 eggs
1 (13 ounce can) evaporated milk
¾ cup sugar
½ teaspoon salt
¼ teaspoon cinnamon
¼ teaspoon cloves
¼ teaspoon ginger
¼ teaspoon nutmeg   (Continued)

Topping:

½ cup walnuts, chopped
½ cup sugar
2 tablespoon butter softened

In a large bowl, combine flour, oatmeal,
sugar and butter. Mix until crumbly. Press
mixture into a greased 13x9x2 inch pan.
Bake in preheated oven at 350 degrees for
15 minutes.

In a large mixing bowl, combine pumpkin,
eggs, evaporated milk, sugar, and spices.
Mix at medium speed until mixture is smooth.
Pour into crust and bake for 20 minutes.

Meanwhile, in a small bowl, combine walnuts,
sugar and butter. Mix until crumbly. Remove
pan from oven and sprinkle filling with
topping mixture. Continue baking for 30 to
35 more minutes or until filling is set. Cool
thoroughly before removing from pan. Cut in
2 inch squares and serve with a dollop of
whipped cream.

Teenagers

CHAPTER SEVEN PROVERB

"As the twig is bent, so grows the tree"
Alexander Pope

Recipes

Pumpkin Treats for Youngsters

Teenagers and indeed the whole family will enjoy these treats.

- - - - CHAPTER SEVEN - - - -

Teen-Agers

**TEEN KILLS CHILD WHILE
JOY-RIDING IN STOLEN CAR**

**TWO TEENS OPEN FIRE
ON CLASSMATES,
KILLING THIRTEEN**

The newspaper headlines scream stories of horrendous crimes committed by teenagers who seem to have no conscience or sense of right or wrong. These stories are tragic and bewildering because the teenage workers who help us at the farm are terrific and tackle some of the most tedious jobs with enthusiasm; in fact, they add energy and intensity to many tasks. How did these teenagers get to be so terrific? I think I discovered part of the answer to that question one summer while I was supervising our young berry pickers.

We have a pick-your-own strawberry patch, and during the height of the season in June, we need to have some berries picked for our farm market. Teenagers come and earn some spending money by picking berries for a couple of hours in the early morning when it's cool and the berries are at their peak.

Sara was one of our best pickers. Even though she was only thirteen years old, her baskets of berries were always picture perfect.   One morning when Sara's mother brought her to the farm to pick berries, her little brother Zachary came along. Their mother began browsing in the flower market, and Zachary quickly approached me and asked for a job. I looked at him skeptically for he appeared to be only about ten years old. I knew from experience that children don't develop the gentle touch and keen eye of a successful berry picker until at least the age of twelve. However, his sister was an excellent picker and he appeared to be very eager, so I found it impossible to deny his request.

"We usually don't hire people until they are thirteen," I warned him, "But if you would like to show me what you can do, here is a box with which to try."

He grinned from ear to ear, quickly accepted the box and ran to the strawberry field. In about fifteen minutes he returned still smiling and presented his box of berries for inspection. I set the box of berries on the counter and realized that I had a big problem. It contained the worst mess of berries that I had ever seen. Most of his berries had unsightly spots on them. "With a field full of beautiful berries, why did he pick the ones that should have been left for the birds?" I asked myself. "And why did he pick the ones with unripe whitish spots on them instead of the delicious red ones?" It was obvious that he didn't have the 'right stuff' to be a berry picker.

I tactfully tried to show him how this berry had a rotten spot, and that berry was not entirely red, and he immediately tried to pick out the bad ones. As he pushed the berries from side to side in the box, he ruptured the skins of the ripe ones and red juice began to seep from the bottom of the box and trickle across the counter. As he tried to "fix things," his fingers became red and sticky and the berries clung to them and further inhibited his ability to improve the situation. I knew that I must tactfully tell him that he was a failure as a berry picker.

Noticing that her son's first job interview was not going well, Zachary's mother, who had been shopping within hearing distance, stepped forward just as I was about to tell Zac to come back in three years.

Gently, she inserted a suggestion. "Zac, perhaps our family could come and pick strawberries this weekend so that you could practice and then you could come back on Monday and try again. Would that be all right?"

I gladly agreed to the plan because I didn't want to quash his enthusiasm and because I could no longer bear to watch him mutilate my strawberries.

On Monday morning the strawberry pickers lined up for their boxes and Zachary eagerly asked for his second chance. I smiled, handed him a berry box and prayed for a miracle. Fifteen minutes later, he returned from the field and lifted his box for my inspection. I looked at the berries very carefully and breathed a sigh of relief. The strawberries weren't perfect, but it was obvious that this young man had potential.

"Very good, Zachary," I said and he beamed with pride. I proceeded to give him a few helpful hints about berry picking. He listened carefully and then he returned to the field. At the end of the picking session, Zac lined up with the other teenagers to have his berries inspected. When I handed him the four one-dollar bills that he had earned, he nearly burst with happiness.

Over the next three years, I observed Zachary as he became one of our most capable and valued employees. I also observed his mother as she mothered from a distance -- never interfering with his activities, but always enabling him to grow and learn by providing transportation to work and offering praise for jobs well done. I could see that he was secure in the steadfastness of her love and support; and thus, his confidence in his own abilities multiplied.

PUMPKIN PATCH PROVERB:
A Mother's Love can Turn
Failure into Success.

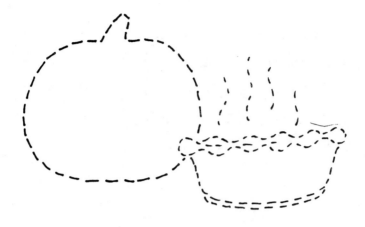

RECYCLING YOUR JACK-O'-LANTERN
(PREPARING FRESH PUMPKIN PULP)

Preparing your own pulp from a small pie or cooking type variety of pumpkin is economical and a terrific learning experience for youngsters. Here is how to do it.

To boil:
Wash and remove stem from pumpkin. Cut in half and scoop out seeds (reserve for roasted seeds) and membranes. You can use your Jack-o'-lantern if it is still firm, but you must cut off any burned portion.

Cut pumpkin into pieces and put into large saucepan. Cover with water. Bring to a boil on high temperature and reduce to low heat for approximately 10 minutes or until pumpkin is tender. Remove from heat, drain liquid, and allow it to cool for handling. Peel skin from pieces. Puree or mash pulp with food mill, sieve, food processor, blender or potato masher. Store in refrigerator or freeze in 1 to 2 cup containers for use with your favorite recipes.

To microwave:
Follow the above boiling directions, substituting an appropriate microwave container. Stir the pieces often to cook evenly.

To bake:
Wash and remove stem from pumpkin. Cut in half and scoop out seeds and membranes. Place halves face down on a baking dish or cookie sheet. Bake in preheated oven at 325 degrees for 45-50 minutes or until tender. Allow to cool before handling. Peel skin off or scoop pulp from skin. Puree or mash the pulp as above.

ROASTING PUMPKIN SEEDS

When carving a Jack-o'-lantern or preparing a cooking variety pumpkin for making pulp, cover the removed insides with water and separate seeds from membranes. Drain seeds and blot dry with paper toweling. Discard membranes.

Basic seasoning after baking:
Spread the seeds evenly on an ungreased cookie sheet. Bake at 375 degrees for 12 minutes or until crisp and lightly browned. Salt to taste.

Spicy seasoning before baking:
Specially packaged seasoning mixes can be added to drained and dried seeds before baking. Self seasoning suggestion include: garlic salt, onion salt, dill weed, dried parsley, Cajun seasoning, lemon pepper, bell pepper, etc. Bake at 325 degrees for 25-30 minutes or until seeds begin to brown and are crisp. Stir often to prevent sticking. Cool before eating.

Seasoning dry roasted seeds:
Coat seeds with one teaspoon light vegetable oil for each cup of seeds. Season before baking and as directed above.

EASY RECIPES FOR KIDS

JOYCE'S PUMPKIN PUDDING
(4-6 servings)
1 cup pure pumpkin
¼ teaspoon salt
½ teaspoon cinnamon
1 tablespoon honey
1 ½ cup milk
1 pkg. instant vanilla pudding (3 ¾ oz.)

In a mixing bowl, combine pumpkin, salt, cinnamon, and honey. Add milk and stir until smooth. Add pudding mix and beat until it begins to thicken. Pour into cups. Chill before serving.

CHOCOLATE PUMPKIN BALLS

2 ½ cups vanilla wafers, crushed
1 cup pecans, ground
½ cup powdered sugar, sifted
1½ teaspoon cinnamon
¼ teaspoon nutmeg
6 ounce semi-sweet mini-chocolate chips
½ cup pure pumpkin
1/3 cup apple juice
¼ cup powdered sugar, sifted

In a medium bowl, combine vanilla wafers, pecans, ½ cup powdered sugar and cinnamon. Blend in chocolate chips, pumpkin and apple juice. With your hands, form teaspoons of mixture into 1-inch balls. Chill until firm. Just before serving, roll balls in ¼ cup of powdered sugar.

Information contributed by:

1. Susan Butler, <u>Butler's Orchard</u>, Germantown, Maryland
2. Barbara Middleton, <u>Middleton Berry Farm</u>, Oakland, Michigan
3. Joyce Fulton, <u>Fulton Farms</u>, Troy, Ohio

Howard the Duck

CHAPTER EIGHT PROVERB

"As you sow,
so shall you reap"
The Bible

Recipes

Munchy Pumpkin Cookies

*Everyone will be sorry when these delicious
cookies are gone.*

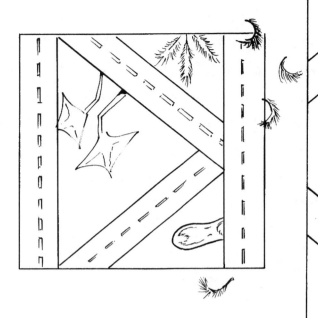

- - - - CHAPTER EIGHT - - - -

Howard the Duck

Howard, the Duck, came to live at our farm the same way that many of our other animals have arrived. Their owners realized that the cute little creature that they loved as a baby had grown up to be a miserable, messy nuisance, and they began calling farms in the area to find an adoptive home.

When Howard's owner called, we were very hesitant about taking another duck because we had a flock of our own that had been together since birth, and we knew that ducks are quite territorial. After pleas and descriptions of the duck's probable fate, we finally consented to take the unwanted pet.

Howard was the ugliest duck that I've ever seen. His huge red-orange feet splayed outward in an awkward waddle. His unkept gray-white and black feathers gave him a perpetual bad-hair-day appearance, and the red jagged marking atop his head made him look like a street fighter. We identified him as a merganzer, but that didn't excuse his ugliness. He immediately became the brunt of all the barnyard unkindness, garnering pecks and pulls whenever he approached the other fowl.

Howard soon resorted to wandering off by himself across the field. He was a pathetic sight, waddling unsteadily about on his oversized webbed feet in search of food. If he even came close to the other birds, he was chased off by a barrage of abuse.

Realizing that Howard led a lonely existence, some of the people on the farm tried to befriend him. Esther, the lady who managed the outdoor market, usually brought bread crumbs for him when she arrived each day. You could see him plod toward her each morning, in all his grotesqueness, and gobble up every crumb that she scattered before him, even though he had eaten a hearty breakfast at sunrise. After feeding Howard, Esther would assume her position behind the counter to conduct the daily business.

One day she arrived a little late and hurried to help a customer at the sales counter. In the midst of helping the customer, she felt a sharp thump, thump, thump on her ankle. Looking down she saw Howard, using his clumsy beak to remind her in no uncertain terms, that he had not received his crumbs. He refused to go away or stop pecking until he got his treats. It seems that Howard had an ugly disposition as well as appearance. Esther continued to bring him crumbs, even after that incident, but more out of the fear of retaliation than love.

Two months later when we found Howard in the middle of the road looking like a pressed duck entree, nobody mourned his death, because he had become a real annoyance to everyone.

PUMPKIN PATCH PROVERB:
    If You Have an
    Ugly Appearance <u>and</u> Disposition,
    Don't Cross the Road.

Recipe from a
Pumpkin Patch
in Rhode Island

NANCY'S PUMPKIN COOKIES
(36 Cookies)

½ cup butter, softened
1½ cup sugar
1 egg
1 cup pure pumpkin
1 teaspoon vanilla
2 ½ cups all-purpose flour
1 teaspoon baking powder
1 teaspoon baking soda
½ teaspoon salt
1 teaspoon cinnamon
1 teaspoon nutmeg
½ cup diced roasted almonds
1 cup chocolate chips

(Continued on next page)

With electric mixer, in large bowl, cream together butter and sugar. Beat in egg, pumpkin, and vanilla until smooth. In a separate bowl, sift together flour, baking powder, baking soda, salt, nutmeg and cinnamon. Mix together all ingredients until well combined. Stir in nuts and chocolate chips. Drop by rounded teaspoons, 2 inches apart onto a lightly greased baking sheet.

Bake in preheated 350 degrees F. oven for 12 to 15 minutes or until browned and center is set.

**Contributed by
Jeanne Jackson,
Iron Kettle Farm,
Candor, NY**

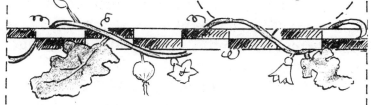

*Recipe from a
Pumpkin Patch
in New York*

SOFT PUMPKIN COOKIES
(36 cookies)

½ cup butter, softened
1-1/2 cup sugar
1 cup pure pumpkin
1 egg
1 teaspoon vanilla
2 ½ cups flour
1 teaspoon baking soda
1 teaspoon baking powder
1 teaspoon cinnamon
½ teaspoon nutmeg
½ teaspoon salt

Optional: 1 cup raisins, nuts,
Or 1 cup quick oatmeal with
½ cup drained pineapple

(Continued on next page)

Glaze:
2 cups powdered sugar
1 teaspoon vanilla
1 tablespoon melted butter
3 tablespoon milk

In a large mixing bowl, cream together butter and sugar. Mix in pumpkin. Add egg and vanilla and beat until fluffy. Sift together flour, baking soda, baking powder, cinnamon, nutmeg, and salt. Slowly combine flour mixture to creamed mixture. Grease cookie sheet and drop teaspoon size amounts evenly on sheet. Bake in preheated oven at 350 degrees for 15-17 minutes. Remove from sheet and cool.

Glaze: In a small mixing bowl, cream together powdered sugar, vanilla, butter, and milk. Spread on cookies. Spread glaze on each cookie.

Contributed by
Helen Huitink
PUMPKINLAND
Orange City, IA

Recipe from a
Pumpkin Patch
in Iowa

PUMPKIN-CHEESE MARBLE TART
(Serves 10-12)

1 cup all-purpose flour
¼ cup pecans or walnuts
¼ cup butter
1 tablespoon shortening
1 egg yolk
1 (8 oz.) package cream cheese
½ teaspoon vanilla
1/3 cup sugar
1 tablespoon all-purpose flour
1 egg
2 tablespoon milk
1 cup pure pumpkin
1/3 cup packed brown sugar
1 teaspoon pumpkin pie spice
¼ cup milk
Whipped Cream, pecans (optional)

In a mixing bowl, combine 1 cup flour, ground nuts, and ¼ tsp. salt. Cut in (cold) butter till mixture resembles course crumbs. Make a well in the center. Beat together egg yolk and 2 Tbsp. water. Add to flour mixture. Stir with fork just until dough forms a ball. Turn onto floured surface and knead 4 times.

On a lightly floured surface roll dough to a circle 11 inches in diameter. Fit in a 10-in. flan pan, pressing bottom and sides gently to remove any air bubbles. Turn overlapping dough to inside and press against edges of pan. Prick sides with fork. Line bottom and sides of pan with double thickness of heavy-duty foil. Bake in preheated 400 degree oven for 10 minutes: remove the foil. Cool on rack.

In mixer bowl, beat cream cheese that has been softened and vanilla until fluffy. Add sugar, 1 Tbsp. flour, and dash of salt; beat till smooth. Add egg; beat just until combined. Do not overmix. Stir in 2 Tbsp milk. Remove ½ cup of mixture. Combine pumpkin, brown sugar and pumpkin pie spice. Stir in reserved cream-cheese mixture and the ¼ cup milk. Spoon pumpkin mixture and remaining cream-cheese mixture into crust. Using a spatula, gently swirl batter to marble. Bake for 25-30 min. in preheated 375 degree oven until set. Cool, remove from pan. Garnish with whipped cream, pecans, or berries.

A Duck of a Different Color

CHAPTER NINE PROVERB

"You Never Know What you Can Do Until you Try"

Unknown

Recipes

Scrumptious Pumpkin Cakes

These Cakes will bring a happy ending to any meal.

- - - - CHAPTER NINE - - - -

A Duck of a
Different Color

ive years after the demise of
Howard, a duck of a different
color came to live at Reilly's Farm.

117

A suburban family called to beg asylum for a fluffy little duck that they had found in their back yard. They were puzzled as to why it was wandering around their yard and where it had come from, because there wasn't a pond for miles around. Mostly they were concerned for its survival because the city ordinance did not allow undomesticated animals. Since most of our ducks were still in their fluffy unfeathered stage, we decided to try to integrate it into the flock.

The family brought the duck to the farm and released it close to the other birds as we watched tentatively. The other ducklings approached the newcomer cautiously. The largest duckling, that was beginning to grow feathers, decided to establish his superiority and came forward to chase the little orphan away. The newcomer was much smaller, but he faced 'Goliath' squarely and grabbed hold of his feathers with his tiny beak and began shaking his head about savagely, even though his little webbed feet were often lifted entirely off the ground by the larger duck's aggressive movements. The little orphan hung on tenaciously despite the pecks until the attacking duckling tired of the game and decided to retreat.

During the course of the day, several other ducklings tried to take on the newcomer but each time one attacked, the orphan stood his ground. Reaching out with his little beak and firmly gripping the attacker's fuzz or feathers, he would shake his head furiously about until the attacker became discouraged and turned away. He truly showed remarkable courage.

After a few days, the other birds accepted the newcomer into the group, and things settled down. The newcomer happily fell in step with the line of ducks as the flock perused the farm looking for bugs and other treats. As the fuzz of the flock turned to feathers, the fluffy little duck developed some distinctive markings and a definitive shape. Much to our surprise the little stray that we had adopted turned into a Canada goose! The wild goose never tried to fly away, but, instead, seemed content to follow his flock of new friends as they foraged for food.

All summer the duck-duck-goose line waddled purposefully about the farm, scooping up insects, snipping off the tender tops of the weeds, swimming in the rain puddles, and enjoying each other's company. They grew quite large and were an impressive-looking group marching from here to there all in step, one after the other.

Autumn arrived. Russet leaves decorated the giant oak trees and the maples stood in a sea of red and gold leaves. The chilly weather didn't impede the activities of the duck flock because they were well insulated by their feathers and down. Since food was becoming scarce, the flock gathered in front of the barn each morning with the other animals for their daily rations.

Finally, winter approached and it was

time to gather up the flock and sell them. Catching the birds was not an easy task for they had grown accustomed to freely roaming the fields. The tall woven-wire fence connected to the barn served as a catching net where the birds could be cornered, and we slowly and carefully herded the fowl toward that barricade.

Some ducks feebly flapped their wings and attempted to escape, but they were eventually squeezed against the fence and hands reached out to gather them up and put them in the cage -- except for the little orphan. When he saw his would-be captors approaching, he flapped his wings furiously and to his surprise and ours, he cleared the fence! He flapped harder and his wings suddenly found great strength and he soared over the barn. We watched this maiden voyage of our little orphan with amazement until he disappeared from sight, probably in search of a new flock of friends; and we wished him Godspeed.

I always look up when a flock of Canada geese goes honking overhead to see if our little orphan is flying somewhere in the V-formation, hoping that he will dip his wing to say hello.

PUMPKIN PATCH PROVERB:
When Push Comes to Shove, FLY!

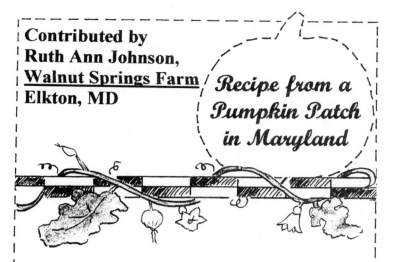

**Contributed by
Ruth Ann Johnson,
Walnut Springs Farm
Elkton, MD**

*Recipe from a
Pumpkin Patch
in Maryland*

RUTH ANN'S
PUMPKIN POUND CAKE
(Serves 12)

1 cup butter or margarine, softened
3 cups sugar
5 large eggs
3 cups all-purpose flour
2 teaspoon baking powder
½ teaspoon baking soda
½ teaspoon salt
2 teaspoon cinnamon
¼ teaspoon cloves
1/8 teaspoon apple pie spice
2 cups pure pumpkin
1/3 cup rum

(Continued on next page)

In a large mixer bowl, beat butter at medium speed about 2 minutes or until soft and creamy. Gradually add sugar beating at medium speed for 5 to 7 minutes. Add eggs, one at a time, beating just until yellow disappears. Sift together flour, baking powder, baking soda, salt, cinnamon, cloves, and apple pie spice.

Combine pumpkin and rum. Add flour mixture to creamed mixture, alternately with pumpkin mixture, beginning and ending with flour mixture. Mix at lowest speed just until blended after each addition. Pour batter into a greased and floured 10-inch tube pan (angel food cake pan). Bake in preheated oven at 325 degrees for 1 hour and 25 to 30 minutes or until toothpick comes out clean. Cool cake in pan on a wire rack 10 minutes; then remove from pan, and let cool.

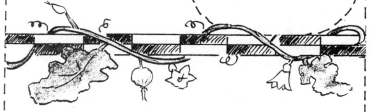

Recipe from a Pumpkin Patch in Pennsylvania

JODY'S PUMPKIN CHEESE CAKE
(8 servings)

Crust:
¾ cup graham cracker crumbs
½ cup ground pecans
2 tablespoons sugar
2 tablespoons brown sugar
¼ cup melted butter

Filling:
¾ cup sugar
¾ cup pure pumpkin
3 egg yolks
1½ teaspoon cinnamon
½ teaspoon nutmeg
½ teaspoon ground ginger
½ teaspoon salt

(Continued on next page)

Cream together:
3 (8-ounce) packages cream cheese
1/3 cup sugar
1 egg
1 egg yolk
2 tablespoons whipping cream
1 tablespoon corn starch
1 teaspoon vanilla extract
½ teaspoon lemon extract

Combine CRUST ingredients. Mix well. Press firmly into a 9" spring form pan.

In a medium bowl, combine ¾ cup sugar, pumpkin, 3 egg yolks, cinnamon, nutmeg, ginger and salt and mix well. Set aside.

In a large bowl, beat cream cheese with an electric mixer until it is light and fluffy. Gradually add the sugar, mixing well. Add egg, egg yolk and whipping cream, beating well. Add cornstarch and extracts, beating until smooth. Add the pumpkin mixture, mixing well.

Pour into the greased spring form pan. Bake in a preheated oven at 350 degrees for 50-55 minutes. Let cool on a wire rack. Store in refrigerator. Chill. Garnish with whipped cream and pecans and raspberries when serving.

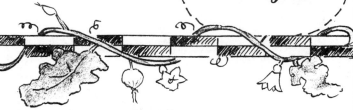

Recipe from a Pumpkin Patch in Virginia

JUDY'S PUMPKIN BUNDT CAKE
(Serves 12)

1 box yellow cake mix
1 box instant butterscotch pudding mix
1 cup pure pumpkin
4 eggs
¼ cup oil
¼ cup water
2 teaspoons pumpkin pie spice
¼ teaspoon pepper
1 teaspoon cinnamon
1 teaspoon vanilla

In a large mixer bowl, add all ingredients. Mix at medium speed for 4 minutes. Pour batter into a greased and floured bundt cake pan. Bake in preheated oven at 350 degrees for 40-45 minutes. Cool for 10 minutes before removing from pan.

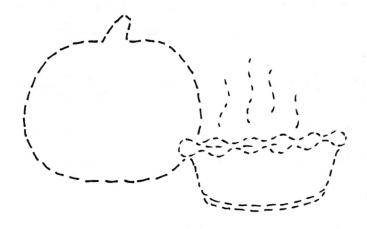

A Night to Remember

CHAPTER TEN PROVERB

"Love Conquers All"
Virgil

Recipes

Warm Pumpkin Soups, etc.

These recipes will make any evening meal a night to remember.

- - - - CHAPTER TEN - - - -

A Night To Remember

Every autumn I invite all of my relatives to come and visit us, and those who accept

131

the invitation are immediately pressed into service at our Harvest Festival as ticket sellers, hot dog cooks, pumpkin haulers, or any other job that needs an able body and a willing spirit. My extended family members have all heard stories about the fun and excitement in the Pumpkin Patch, so they expect to become part of the action when they arrive.

Three years ago my brother, Jerry, found time to visit, and we eagerly welcomed him -- not just because he was my brother, but because he possessed a talent that was very much in demand in October -- he was a tractor driver! He happily accepted the prestigious position, and all day long he ferried people out to and back from the Pumpkin Patch. A broad smile adorned his face, and he seemed to be having as much fun as the people riding on his wagon.

At the end of the day, we closed down the pumpkin-picking activities and prepared for the nighttime group hayrides.

Church groups, scout groups, friends and families had made reservations for an hour hayride around our country roads which concluded at a picnic site with a blazing bonfire. At that site the group could spend the rest of the night enjoying the camaraderie of song and s'mores and watching the children make glow worms out of marshmallow sticks. Most of the children wore themselves out long before the eleven o'clock curfew by playing flashlight tag and scaring each other in the darkness.

As soon as the daytime activities closed, my husband, Mike, began coordinating the night hayrides and assigning tractor drivers to the various groups listed in the reservation book. Since this was Jerry's first night hayride, Mike decided to assign him a very special young couple. Usually the groups consist of about 35 people, but this young man wanted to propose marriage to his girlfriend in a romantic manner and he thought an old-fashioned hayride would be the perfect vehicle.

The young man arrived with an engagement ring in his pocket and a box containing a bottle of champagne and glasses with which to celebrate the occasion. He surreptitiously concealed the box in the hay so that he could bring it out at the appropriate moment. From here on, I will try to relate the events of the evening in a manner that will help you appreciate what was occurring in the hearts and minds of those on the tractor and on the wagon; so that you can fully understand why this was truly a night to remember for all concerned.

Jerry met his romantic young couple and helped them onto the wagon. As they were getting settled, Mike gave Jerry some last minute instructions.

"Follow the road around the perimeter of the farm -- there's really only one road so you shouldn't have a problem. Drop the couple at the picnic site after you pass the big barn. We'll light the bonfire at that site just before you arrive. Go slowly because the ride is supposed to last about an hour. If you have any trouble, just call me on the CB. You're driving the big blue tractor so your CB handle is Big Blue. Any questions?"

Jerry shook his head, gave Mike the thumbs up sign, climbed up to the cab of the tractor and the rig disappeared into the night. The lovebirds had already snuggled down in the soft, fragrant hay. As the tractor crept around a bend, Jerry was taken aback!

THOUGHTS ON THE TRACTOR : "What's that up ahead? A fork in the road? I thought Mike said there was only one road? This place certainly looks different at night than it did in the daylight. Which way should I go? I know the farm is mainly off to the left, so I think I'd better go left."

THOUGHTS ON THE WAGON: "Oh, what a night! Those stars are so close we can almost touch them! What a great idea this was! A sky full of stars, a sliver of a moon, my loved one beside me! It doesn't get any better than this! This magical moment certainly calls for a kiss."

Jerry turned slowly to the left; and as he proceeded, he began to suspect that he had taken the road less traveled, because it narrowed to a mere path.

THOUGHT ON THE TRACTOR: "My headlights are telling me that I'm running out of road! Where in the heck am I? None of this looks familiar. I'm afraid I'm going to have to do something that I try to avoid at all costs - something that goes counter to my nature. I'm going to have to ask for directions! I'll turn the CB down very low so that the couple can't hear it."

Jerry turned down the volume of the CB so that only he could hear it, but before he could say a word, a voice came over the radio. "Base calling Big Blue. Come in, please. Walter said he saw lights out in the pumpkin field. Is that you? Give me your position."

"This is Big Blue," Jerry replied, "You tell **me** where the heck I am! And how do I get out of here?"

"Base calling Big Blue. I can see your headlights now. You're heading for the field that we just plowed. It's going to get very bumpy in a few minutes! Turn to the right and traverse the field. If you cross it at a slant, it will be less bumpy. When you get to the other side of the field, you'll see the road again going off to the left. Gear down and go really slow."

THOUGHTS ON THE WAGON: "Oh, how could this night be more perfect! The endless starry sky overhead. The night air whispering around our bed of hay. The wagon rocking my love and me gently as we're locked in an embrace. This definitely calls for a kiss."

MEANWHILE, BACK ON THE TRACTOR: "Big Blue calling base. I've been bumping across this field forever! How far did you say it was? Those people on the wagon must feel like a couple of scrambled eggs by now! Oh, wait ! I see the edge of the field! Now which way did you say to go?"

Jerry was greatly relieved to see a real road, and he turned left after reaching it.

MEANWHILE BACK ON THE WAGON: " I could go on like this forever, my love, but let's sit up for a moment. I have a very important question to ask you. Will you marry me? Yes? Yes! Give me your hand. (He reached into his pocket and brought out the ring.) This ring is a sign of my undying love. I will cherish you always. This calls for a celebration!" He lifted up the champagne and glasses that were sequestered beneath the hay, and popped the cork, "But first, a kiss would be appropriate."

THOUGHTS ON THE TRACTOR: "I'm a nervous wreck! I'm already ten minutes late in dropping these two off! What was that noise? Did I hear a tire on the wagon pop? That's all I need, a flat tire! Well, I don't care, I'm not stopping! I'm dragging this rig home on a rim and a prayer! How am I going to explain to this guy why I pulled him and his girlfriend across a plowed field for half an hour? Maybe I should just apologize and offer to give him his money back. It wouldn't unspoil his romantic evening, but at least he wouldn't feel cheated. Thank God, there's the bonfire! What a miserable night!"

Jerry stopped the tractor beside the bonfire and the young man helped his new fiancee down from the wagon. As Jerry climbed down from the cab of the tractor, he definitely decided that a simple confession and offer of reimbursement would be the best course to follow. He was searching for the right words when the young man turned to him and enthusiastically blurted out, "Thanks for that wonderful hayride; it couldn't have been more perfect!" and he thrust a $5 tip into Jerry's hand.

PUMPKIN PATCH PROVERB:
We See the World From the Inside Out.

Contributed by
<u>**Lyman Orchards**</u>
<u>**Farm Market**</u>
Middlefield, CT

Recipe from a
Pumpkin Patch
in Connecticut

PUMPKIN HARVEST SOUP
(Serves 4)

1 cup milk
1 onion, thinly sliced
1 bay leaf
1 cup chicken broth
1 cup pure pumpkin
1 ½ tablespoon melted butter
1 ½ tablespoon flour
½ teaspoon salt
Dash white pepper

In a medium saucepan, combine milk, onions,
and bay leaf. Slowly bring to a boil. Strain,
then combine strained ingredients with the
chicken broth and pure pumpkin (save milk).

(Continued on next page)

In a separate saucepan, make a roux by combining the butter with the flour and cooking over low heat for 5 minutes to avoid the floury taste. Slowly add the milk mixture to the roux and whisk until the soup is smooth. Add pumpkin–chicken mixture to the milk mixture. Add salt and pepper to taste. Simmer over low heat an additional 5 minutes to allow flavors to develop.

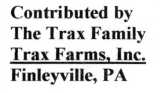

**Contributed by
The Trax Family
<u>Trax Farms, Inc.</u>
Finleyville, PA**

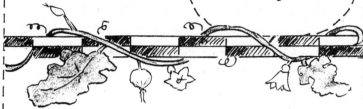

*Recipe from a
Pumpkin Patch
in Pennsylvania*

DINNER-IN-A-PUMPKIN

1 (8-10 lb.) Trax Farm pumpkin
1-1/2 ground beef
1 small onion, chopped
1 clove garlic, minced
1-1/2 teaspoon sugar
1-1/2 teaspoon Italian herbs
1-1/2 teaspoon salt
¼ teaspoon pepper
4 cups tomato juice
3 cups cabbage
½ lb. green beans
1 cup rice, uncooked

(Direction on next page)

Wash pumpkin, cut off top and scrape out seeds and discard. Cook ground beef slightly; drain off fat. Add onion and garlic, saute lightly. Add seasonings and tomato juice; heat. Mix with uncooked rice. Shred cabbage and cut green beans. Layer 1/3 each of the cabbage, green beans, rice, and meat mixture in the pumpkin. Repeat layers and replace lid. Place in 350 degrees oven and bake for 2 ½ to 3 hours or until done. Pumpkin is done when it is soft when pierced with a fork. Serve with tossed green salad and cornbread.

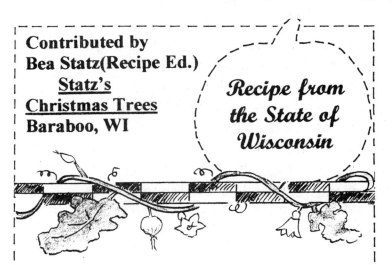

Contributed by
Bea Statz(Recipe Ed.)
Statz's
Christmas Trees
Baraboo, WI

*Recipe from
the State of
Wisconsin*

PUMPKIN ORANGE SOUP
(Makes 4 servings)

2 tablespoons butter, divided
1 small onion, finely chopped
2 cups orange juice
1 ¾ cup (15 ounce can) pure pumpkin
1 cup milk
¾ cup chicken broth, canned or homemade
1 teaspoon grated orange peel
1 teaspoon ginger
½ teaspoon salt
1/8 teaspoon white pepper
4 orange slices, for garnish
¼ cup pumpkin seeds, for garnish

(Continued on next page)

In large saucepan, melt 1 tablespoon butter on medium heat; saute onion until soft. Stir in orange juice, pumpkin, milk, chicken broth, orange peel, ginger, salt and pepper. Bring to a simmer, covered, on medium heat for 10 minutes. Meanwhile, in small saucepan melt remaining 1 tablespoon butter; saute pumpkin seeds until lightly toasted. Drain on paper towel. Spoon soup into warm bowls. Garnish with orange slices and toasted pumpkin seeds.

ABOUT THE ILLUSTRATIONS

Professor Carol Stavish's illustrations were inspired by the following quilt patterns and stitches:

Story

How Do You Choose a Pumpkin?
Quilt Pattern: Round and Round

The Grouch
Quilt Pattern: Rail Fence

Cool
Quilt Pattern: Blazing Star

Choices
Quilt Pattern: Wedding Ring

Sir Thomas Turkey, Esquire
Quilt Pattern: King's Cross

Teengers
Quit Pattern: Tumbling Blocks

Howard the Duck
Quilt Pattern: Irish Chain

A Night to Remember
Quilt Pattern: Four Patch

STITCHES

Running stitch   — — — — — — —

Stippling

Mennonite Tack

Crow's Feet   < < < < < <

Cross Stitch   X X X X X X X

French Knot

Running Tie

Whip Stitch

Slip Stitch

Pumpkin Seed Design

148

Contributors Information

Carolyn Beinlich, Triple B Farms
823 Berry Lane, Monongahela, PA 15063

Susan Butler, Butler's Orchard.
22200 Davis Mill Rd. Germantown, MD 20876

Judy Fulks, Belvedere Plantation
1601 Belvedere Drive, Fredericksburg, VA 22408

Joyce Fulton, Fulton Farms,
1709 State Route 202, Troy, OH 45373

Beverly Huber Engleman, Joe Huber's Farm,
2421 Scotville Rd., Borden, IN 47106

Helen Huitink, PUMPKINLAND,
4123 Jackson Avenue, Orange City, IA 51041

Jeanne Jackson, Iron Kettle Farm,
707 Owego Rd., Rt. 96, Candor, NY 13743

Mary Jacobson, Pine Tree Apple Orchards,
450 Orchard Rd., White Bear Lake, MN 55110

Ruth Ann Johnson, Walnut Springs Farm,
3910 Blue Ball Rd., Elkton, MD 21921

Barbara Middleton, Middleton Berry Farm,
2120 Stoney Creek Farm, Oakland, MI 48363

Diane Patterson, Lyman Orchards Farm Market.
Rte. 147 & 157, Middlefield, CT, 06455

Nancy Schartner, Schartner Farms,
Rt.2 & One Arnold Place, Exeter, RI, 02822

Teresa Schmitt, F & W Schmitt Pumpkin Farm,
Exit 49 & South Long Island Expressway,
Walt Whitman Road, Melville, NY 11747

Bea Statz, Statz's Christmas Trees,
10675 N. Reedsburg Rd., Baraboo, WI 53913

Linda Struye, The Little Farmer,
N9438 Hwy 151, Malone, WI 53049

The Trax Family, Trax Farms, Inc.
528 Trax Road, Finleyville, PA 15332

Sunday G. Todosciuk, Andy T's Farms,
3127 & 3131 S. US 27, St. John's, MI 48879